The Courage to Grow Old

The Courage to Grow Old

Barbara Cawthorne Crafton

Morehouse Publishing
NEW YORK · HARRISBURG · DENVER

Unless otherwise noted, the Scripture quotations contained herein are from the New Revised Standard Version Bible, copyright © 1989 by the Division of Christian Education of the National Council of Churches of Christ in the U.S.A. Used by permission. All rights reserved.

Morehouse Publishing, 4785 Linglestown Road, Suite 101, Harrisburg, PA 17112

Morehouse Publishing, 19 East 34th Street, New York, NY 10016

Morehouse Publishing is an imprint of Church Publishing Incorporated.
www.churchpublishing.org

Cover design by Laurie Klein Westhafer
Typeset by Rose Design

Library of Congress Cataloging-in-Publication Data

A catalog record of this book is available from the Library of Congress.

ISBN-13: 978-0-8192-2910-6 (pbk.)
ISBN-13: 978-0-8192-2911-3 (ebook)

Printed in the United States of America

Contents

For Q,
Younger than springtime.

Preface

This amuses me: the first edition of my first book, published twenty years ago, had my picture on the cover—in my early forties, big hair. Ten years later, so did another one: me in my garden, my hair blonde, now, and less of it. I was holding a tray of freshly-baked bread (it was a cookbook). And now here I am again, an old cover girl with jowls, crows feet at the corners of my eyes, a modest wattle adorning my throat. Several years ago I decided it was okay to get old and grey now, instead of old and blonde, and that process is well underway. If I haven't gone home to Jesus ten years from now, maybe we can do another book cover. *Notes From the Nursing Home*, maybe, or *One Foot in the Grave*.

And if I have gone to Jesus? *Spoiler Alert: How It Ends*. That's a great title.

Except that I don't believe that it does end. This life schools us for our opening up to a reality of which hardly any of us are equipped even to dream. Interestingly, it is physicists who seem to be leading us in its direction. Makes me wish I'd taken Physics in school.

But I am excited about it. Interesting: excited about dying, but eager to live. Don't want to leave, but can't wait to see what's out there when I do. So stay tuned: I'll let you know if I can.

Meanwhile, time marches on here. What everyone exclaims about is so true: life is really, really short. We don't have time to waste—however long you may live, today is the only today you will ever have. When it is over, it will be over, and it will not come again. *Don't blow it off!* Don't waste a moment of it wishing you were younger than you are, or that you looked like you used to look, or had done something other than what you did in life. There's no time for that now. Take whatever you have to work with and make today as sweet as you can make it. Nobody can do it for you, and nobody will. It is yours alone.

bcc+
The Geranium Farm
2014

1

The O Word

I'll be sixty-five, my friend said, leaning across the table and dropping her voice to a whisper on the last three syllables, as if she'd just told me she had a venereal disease. I remember her face as she said it, her trapped look, a mixture of panic and shame. I was younger than she and much younger than I am now. I stifled a feeling of annoyance and tried to look sympathetic. I did not intend to call the funeral home when I reached my sixties. Now I'm solidly there, and I still don't. Come to think of it, though, prearrangement *is* a good idea—maybe I will give them a call. But I digress.

What's good about getting old? somebody asked a movie star whose name I cannot recall. *Nothing*, she snapped. I was sorry to hear it. I could think of many good things about getting old. Again, I was much younger than she. But I'm not now, and I still can.

My friend Frank cries into his beer most evenings about not being young anymore. A song from the fifties, the death of a matinee idol—it doesn't take much to send him into the depths. He longs for his lost youth the way a thirsty man longs for water. Nothing in the present holds any delight for him at all, not that I can see. What future there is looks like a prison sentence. With time served, he wonders, how much longer does he have?

I know a lot more about physical vulnerability than I did when I was young. I know that things can't stay the same, not ever—if your well-being depends on never losing anything you currently have, you're in deep trouble. But I also know that people don't have to be full of despair about the incontrovertible fact of their aging, and that the way to continue in peace for the duration is to accept the reality of what is happening to your body and your brain. Hiding from it makes it larger in your imagination than it really is. It fills you with fear of the future, and prevents you from enjoying the world you actually live in right now.

I'm not old! a beautiful woman at a party tells us all defiantly. By that she means that she is not any of the negative things we think old people are: useless, weak, unlovely, alone. But she *is* old—she's eighty-one. Why does she accept a stereotype—one which clearly does not fit her—as the only way there is of being old? Why should anyone? Isn't that a little like saying *I'm not a woman,* when what you mean is *I'm not fragile, overly emotional, unintelligent or timid?* And why, in accepting such stereotypes, should she deny herself the honor of being esteemed for what she is: beautiful, experienced and wise? She has lived much more of her life on earth than she has yet to live—why should she let the negative categories of aging be the only categories that count?

And I am not talking about the freaks of nature you see in vitamin ads, about old people who look like young people. The physical characteristics of an aging body are not the same as those of a young one: does it follow that the word "beautiful" can only apply to the second, never to the first? I have loved my husband's gnarly hands for many years—now my own hands are getting to be that way, tendons and blue veins standing in high relief against new decliv-ities in the backs of them. My eyelids are pleated now—I think they make me look a little sly, as if I knew something most people don't know. Small wrin-kles have appeared around my lips, and two larger ones lead from my nose to the corners of my mouth. When I smile, a dozen lines appear around my eyes and a few more crinkle my cheeks. They remain for a bit after the smile has disappeared, the afterglow of my laugh. Every time I catch sight of them, I see both my present and my future: the lines will multiply and deepen. Soon, they will become a permanent part of my facial topography, whether I am smiling or not! What I do not see is the uneventful landscape of my girlhood face, the face before decades of smiles layered themselves upon it. I have photographs of that young face—it's pretty enough, I suppose. It looks a little blank to me from here, though.

There are other lines. The two vertical ones between my eyebrows that *really* make me look like I know something, and the horizontal parallels on my forehead. They are from furrowing my brow. From thinking hard. Probably also from yelling at people, or at least from wishing I could yell at someone. From tilting my head and raising my eyebrows inquiringly because of something I have not understood, or from being told something whose veracity I have doubted. You can get this stuff Botoxed out of your life for a few months if you want to, but you must be willing to bet that nothing will come up during that time that will require you to look quizzical or wise, and life is just not like that.

From the folds of my eyelids and the crinkles around their corners, my eyes will continue to look out at the world. Unless I lose my sight. Nearsighted since seventh grade, I am used to changes in my vision, and there will be more. One or more of a few cataclysmic things might happen to my eyes, some fixable and some not. Perhaps I'll have to use an electronic reader to magnify my text many times over. I'll be annoyed that I must do so, but I will also be glad that there are such things. It may be that a time will come when no machine can help me see, and that will be hard to bear. I imagine myself going over memories of faces in my mind, memories of art and buildings, memories of the way trees and flowers and the moon looked when I could see them. I imagine myself needing help to navigate my way around my own room, and I imagine myself asking for it. Even if I do go blind, those who gaze into my eyes will see the same blue they have always seen. Maybe a bit lighter. In time, probably, a white ring will surround the blue; if it does, it will remain until my eyes close for the last time.

But wait—here's something else to ponder: there may not be anybody gazing into my eyes! I may well be solitary. I will have friends and I will have my children and grandchildren, but it may well be that I will not have sustained intimacy with anyone in my generation. I may have people who are intimate with my body in ways no one is now, ways no one has been since I was a baby, people who help me do the ordinary things I now do myself without thinking twice: people who help me bathe, eat, dress. I may have people who change my diaper so that I can be fresh and clean. Imagining it now, I feel myself wanting them to be people who love me already, but it is likely that at least some of them will just be people whose job it is to provide such care. I am accustomed to nursing homes; I visit lots of them. No, they're not luxury spas. But they are staffed, for the most part, by decent people who do the best they can for their charges. If my children think it's best for me to be cared for in one, I'll go willingly. If they can't face it—and that may be, as they haven't spent as much time in them as I have—I may insist on it myself.

What I will not do is what I have seen too many other people do: extract a promise from my children or my spouse never to put me in one. People do this when they're young and strong and there's nothing wrong with them. They reiterate the demand every now and then throughout their lives so that nobody forgets, trapping their children into years of unworkable arrangements focused around keeping a promise made without a context. Don't bind your children forever to the things you were afraid of when you were forty because of something you saw or heard about when you were ten—trust them to make decisions based on what's really going on when you're eighty-seven. Have a relationship with them that gives you confidence that they will have your best interest at heart. And here you have more reason to be of good cheer than you may think you have: I have seen many adult children rise to the occasion of their parents' final illness, even when the relationship was not at all an easy one. If yours is truly hopeless though—and some relationships just are—find someone else to fill that role. *And find that person before you need her.* Your own nursing care crisis should not be the first time you've given the matter any thought.

Another thing: whether or not you want to do this cannot be the central question. *Of course* you don't want to enter a nursing home—you'd rather be strong, healthy and live forever. But that option is not for sale, and "I don't want to" isn't much of an argument in the face of the medical and practical needs you may have. We are not children, and part of being an adult is taking responsibility for yourself. In growing older, that means planning concretely for decisions to be made when I can no longer make them, and placing myself in the setting from which it will be easiest for those I love to implement those decisions. Making someone with a full-time job and teenagers in the house fly back and forth to Florida dozens of times a year because you didn't want to move nearer her when you were strong enough to do so is just selfish. Think ahead, and don't do it—our children don't owe us the sacrifice of their own children's well-being. *Honor thy father and thy mother* doesn't mean enabling our parents' denial of the facts of their lives.

And another—why should we live in stubborn and fruitless denial of the facts about *ourselves*, about the death that lies nearer at hand every day we live? Why won't we even talk about it? Why do we think it's better to look right through the physical challenges of the dying, as if we didn't see them, rather than to acknowledge their existence and simply say we're sorry about them? As hospice chaplains and nurses well know, the ones among us who are near their time don't want to waste precious energy helping their families pretend they're not dying. It may be that I will have things I need to tell the ones I leave behind—that will be easier if we can all admit that I'm leaving.

In order to help those who love me deal with my death, I must come to terms with it myself. It will help to think about death in advance. Trust me, this gets easier to do with practice—those things of which we refuse to think don't disappear meekly in response to our refusal: they go underground. There they grow in apparent size and virulence, becoming larger and more unthinkable than they really are. What will happen to me in my death is that I will join the billions of human beings who have died; everyone who has ever lived has managed to do this. We do not die interminably; we die once, and then it is over. Those left behind are haunted by the memory of losing us, but we are not. We pass through a portal of which we are afraid, but then we are through it. Even if the most committed atheist were right, and there were nothing save the life in which we now live, that life would still be over when we die. Death would not hold us suspended between the worlds. We would be gone from this world and its fears.

It will help us to contemplate the fact that death will happen to us. At the very least, we will be less surprised, and the energy shock which so quickly takes from us will be that much more available to us. We will need it for the journey upon which we embark. Dying people don't have abundant energy, and most of what they do have is focused on their departure from this life.

But they do still love the ones they love. Though they haven't much left to give them, one thing they do have is the capacity to leave this world honestly and in a spirit of trust in the ongoingness of existence, with gratitude for the life they were given and a sense of completion. You and I have this capacity, and can leave those we love this final picture of ourselves, if we will have the courage to prepare for our own decline and death while we can. Sometimes I will need the help of those who love me in the project of doing this, for nobody looks death steadily in the face—from time to time, the bravest among us avert our eyes. Sometimes my energy will be consumed by physical pain or a spasm of sorrow. But at times like those, the witness of people I love to the fact that the whole of my life had meaning will balance the difficulty of my leaving it. It will have to. It will be all I have left.

2

Baby, You Can Drive My Car

The campaign to divest him of the car keys was gently fought, but of long duration. There had been a few accidents. He was known to the local police—one time he rear-ended somebody and left the scene: the man he hit followed him home and cornered him in his driveway. To this day, he does not understand why doing that got everyone so riled. Finally, he totaled the car in a snowy encounter with a telephone pole on the day after Christmas. She remains unconvinced that this was due in any way to senility, though one might reasonably have questioned his decision to drive at all on a day like that one.

There was now no car. They decided not to replace it: she commuted to New York by train, and could reach the airport by train when she had to travel. He could take the senior bus. There were taxis. She had her old Schwinn. They lived within walking distance of the grocery store and everything else they needed.

For a year and more it was fine. But then she changed jobs, and suddenly she needed wheels. They walked into a car dealership and bought the first one they saw. Neither of them enjoys shopping.

There are still buses and trains and taxis, as many as there ever were. But they find that they use the car by default, now that they have one. She drives him places, and then she fetches him home. Sometimes he will catch a lift home, with someone who happens to be going that way.

But sometimes—very rarely and, she has now re-promised her children, never again—she has given in to the demands of her own schedule. She has cut her walking time to the train too close, and has allowed him to drive her there and then drive the half mile back home. She has allowed him to drive home from church a few times, when she knew she would be held there longer than he wanted to stay. She promises she will not do this again. She will allow herself the time she needs to manage the chauffeuring. She won't let her own lack of planning put him or anyone else in danger.

But what about him? I have sat in the living rooms of many families, strategizing with them about how to handle the dilemma of a father whose ability to drive is compromised, in the opinion of everyone but him. He turns to me and speaks angrily of his independence, hoping for my support. His grown children argue, lecture, hide the car keys. His wife sits, paralyzed, caught between warring duties to husband and children, afraid to let him drive and afraid not to.

He remembers his parents' car—it had a running board. He remembers his own first car. He remembers taking his young children out to wash the car in the creek, driving it right into the shallow water and soaping it up, then pouring pot after pot of clean water over it while the kids waded in the water and jumped from the rocks. He remembers the road trips they took, how he used to argue with his wife about reading the roadmap, how they would stop to let the kids pee along the side of the road, remembers the motels, the roadside picnic tables. He remembers turning into his own driveway after another day at work. He remembers his first automatic transmission. He remembers when seat belts first appeared in cars.

The children win the war. He stops driving. The car sits in the garage. He goes out to check the oil sometimes, opens the door, slides into the driver's seat.. He sits there for a while. Just sits—they have the keys, his children. He's not going anywhere.

This man I remember well, his anger, his eventual resignation. But I also remember the man who drove his car through the plate glass window of the convenience store on Main Street, seriously injuring the owner's wife. I remember the elderly priest who drove the wrong way up a highway exit ramp, killing himself and the parents of two young teenagers in an oncoming car. I remember an old lady whom I did not know, upside down and still belted in her flipped car—dead before I got to her with the last rites. An automobile is a complicated and powerful piece of machinery. Driving one cannot be simply a matter of one's right to be autonomous. Sometimes it is a matter of life and death.

It didn't have to be this way. The short-sighted postwar decision, on both federal and state levels, to put all our transportation eggs in the automobile's basket quickly eliminated the majority of our train routes nationwide. Manhattan is the one American place in which owning a car is literally more trouble than it's worth—everywhere else, lacking one is a tremendous handicap, adding hours to the days of low-paid workers who must rely on infrequent buses for their commute. Poor people pay for our love affair with cars, yes, but so do the elderly: where there is adequate public transportation people can still travel independently and inexpensively when they should no longer drive, but that is almost nowhere in the United States.

It would just be so inconvenient, my friend says. *I like to be able to go whenever I want to. And taxis are so expensive.*

Well, but so is insurance and car payments and repairs. It would take a lot of taxi rides to add up to what a car owner spends on his wheels. Besides, you walk more. A lot more. And we haven't even discussed parking—it costs $28 a day in Chelsea as I write this, and $40 in midtown. Again, you really do not want to keep a car here.

It is true that people who don't own cars must plan ahead a bit—they must consult the train schedule, factor in the slowness of a bus ride as compared with driving a car. And it is true that using public transportation means that one will sometimes be inconvenienced by other people's actions, though the same holds true when one sits helplessly in a traffic jam. But it is also true that people who are too old to drive are usually also not working full-time—their schedules are less crowded than when they were younger. They can afford a more leisurely pace. They can come to treasure that slowness, so different from the jam-packed days of yore. Perhaps it is time to lose the habit of hurrying, if it's no longer necessary. Perhaps it's time to rediscover the discipline of planning ahead a bit. What's the rush?

Go to Europe. Gasoline is very expensive there, and many people of all ages do not own cars. But they travel anywhere they want to go, using train and bus systems that put ours to shame. Their life expectancy is longer than ours, perhaps because they walk on errands nearer their homes. You may travel great distances in your car, but from your body's point of view, all you're doing when you drive is sitting.

The battles over our driving bring home an important truth: somewhere along the line, all of us must graduate from the adolescent conviction that everything we want to do boils down to a matter of our own civil rights. One's autonomy is important, but it is never absolute. Over and over again, as we age, we stumble upon occasions in which we must decide whether or not to allow our juniors to mentor us. This disagreeable shock is necessary to the survival of the species: their emancipation depends on our willingness to step out of the spotlight when it is time, and it is unreasonable to assume that we will know when that time has arrived. For as long as they possibly can, people deny the truth of the things they don't want to face.

Truth to tell, the time to stop driving is *before* you can no longer do so. You could, of course, wait until you had injured or killed somebody's child—then you could be absolutely sure it was time. But you're sure your reflexes are fine? Good for you. And so you imagine that all those people who have killed or injured themselves or others while driving already knew they weren't up to the task when they left home? No. No, they all thought they were fine, too. So if somebody who loves you tells you it's time to stop, ask yourself this question: Is this a person who wishes me ill? Wants me to be unhappy? Is this someone who has it in for me?

Or is this someone who loves me, and has therefore summoned the courage to tell me an unwelcome truth?

Use buses, trains and taxis. Walk. Hitch a ride with a friend. Factor in the time it will take to do so. Plan ahead. Accept the inconvenience of this new— well, it's old, really—way of living for what it is: this is inconvenience, not tragedy. And do not accept the easy equation of driving with personal power—they have little to do with each other. Not driving will not infantilize you.

Unless you have already decided it will.

3

An Affair to Remember

Dating? You say the word, and it sounds so silly, applied to you. Dating is a young girl with a ponytail and a boy with a crew cut. Dating is a drink after work with somebody interesting-looking, two sharp young people at the top of their game out for an evening, assessing each other once in a while, with no particular urgency in that assessment—life is endless, they know. They've got all the time in the world.

You don't go to work now. You're retired. You are not sure if you're interesting-looking or not. You suspect not. Lately, in fact, you have wondered if you might not somehow have become invisible without knowing it.

Also, things have changed since you last did this. Oh sure, your children think there was no premarital sex in those days, and you've never felt called upon to correct them. Besides, you're not sure that what went on back then—so furtive, so hasty it still embarrasses you to think about it—would be recognizable as sex today anyway, and you'll be damned if you're going to explain it to them.

You don't know how to date. You can tell right now you're not going to be any good at it. You only know how to be married.

Nonetheless, here you are somehow, with plans for the evening. Plans! *The stars / are gonna twinkle and shine / this evening / about a quarter to nine*—you hum the tune to yourself as you get dressed. Except you're not going to meet at a quarter to nine—you're usually in bed by ten. You make up a private new verse, one for old people dating: *No stars / the sun is high up in heaven / I'll see you / about a quarter to seven.*

It's not the same.

Dressing for the evening has not been so fraught in years. When you were married, you each knew what the other looked like naked. You had gotten dressed together for decades. Together you had traveled all the way from "Are my seams straight?" to "Does this pantsuit make me look fat?" So much was automatic, all those years: the tie-straightening, the practiced reach from the passenger seat to brush a bit of lint from a shoulder. You always kept a packet of lens wipes in your purse because he never cleaned his driving glasses. You always carried a comb because she never remembered to put one in when she changed purses. After rejecting a few, you settle on an ensemble and check your look in the mirror. Neither Rock Hudson nor Doris Day looks back at you. *Oh, brother.*

Your date is not a stranger. You are not even sure your date will realize that this is a date. So maybe it isn't. Maybe it's just two friends having dinner and going to a movie afterwards. But you are undeniably excited to be going—so maybe it is a date. You'll just have to wait and see. But you won't have to wait long: it's six-fifteen.

Choosing a restaurant was unexpectedly difficult. Not one you used to go to—oh, no. Not one all your friends go to, either: a new one. Does your date like Italian food? You should have asked. Better have a backup restaurant. That steak place? Maybe. But you are on Lipitor. Should you have asked about that? *Are you on Lipitor?* But you don't ask a question like that on a first date.

This is just too hard. You promise yourself never to go on a date again.

But Italian is fine. A gin and tonic makes you feel better about having embarked on this project, a little stronger. You look across the table at your date and remember that your date is about as old as you are. On balance, you are glad you came. It's not dark out, but it is dusk now, and the dim light is kind to both of you. You say something funny and you both laugh.

You recall, though, that in real life you are not all that funny, and decide against a second gin and tonic.

The movie theater isn't far from the restaurant, so you walk there. Nobody holds hands and nobody offers or takes an arm, which was something you had wondered about, as you are now wondering about how to end the evening. Kiss or no kiss? You have chosen a film without much in the way of sex scenes, and you sit there in the darkness watching it together, your arms touching occasionally on the narrow arm-rests. This is the extent of your physical contact for the evening, but even your elbow notes the touch of another elbow. You realize that you have not wanted to think about how physical your loneliness has been. You make bold to touch your date's forearm with your hand in order to say something about what is happening on the screen, and your date does not recoil. This is where we came in, you say at the end of the film, and your date gets the joke. It is a joke from another era. Maybe you are sort of funny, after all. The kiss at the end of the evening is just on the cheek, but it involves a brief hug.

You see each other again. And again. The time comes when you do make love, and that time arrives a lot sooner than it would have fifty years ago. The chastity maintenance project that preoccupied you and all your friends back then has receded into history—it has been replaced by a troubling concern with what you will look like to each other in the morning. You awaken on the day before the night on which you're pretty sure it's going to happen, and your haggard morning face appalls you. Your body, too: you resemble none of the people in the films you've been seeing together, which have gotten steadily sexier since that first one.

You remember the charity that grew in your marriage as you both aged. It was possible to see earlier eras in a face that no longer looked as it had looked in the sixties—no, not just possible, it was easy. You remember the way you saw the eyes and not the wrinkles around them. You do remember some other thoughts, too, some less charitable critiques of your love, but you remember also that a glance in your own mirror more than sufficed to put them in their place. *Pig!* you say to yourself as you remember this, and *Pig!* your love would have agreed, and you both would have laughed.

How different it is when it happens! And yet how familiar, which it cannot be, can it? But of course it can: you are you, after all. The moment is full of what you know. But it is also full of what someone else knows, someone who was schooled in love differently. And it is two bodies no longer in their prime. You ask awkward questions: Do you like this? What about this? And they are not awkward, once you have asked them. They are generous, sweet questions about how to please. Fifty years ago you did not know how to ask about these things.

Your body is not the one you had back then. It is more intelligent than it used to be, but it is also less responsive to your wishes. Good Lord, you think, how athletic love was in those days! You may still wish you had the body you had then, but you are glad you finally know how to ask about what you do not know.

Time goes by. Holidays. You meet each other's friends, each other's startled children. You vacation together. Then you begin to notice something about yourself: you keep trying to turn this new person into your mate. You keep trying to act married, when you are not married. And then you reverse yourself, and keep trying to get away. Actually, you both do *both* these things at different times. You expect your new love to know what your old love knew, and of course that cannot be. Your new love assumes you will want something you do not want, and it annoys you. It annoys you beyond what it should. It occurs to you that this may not be your new love after all: this may have been just a moment in your life.

This is disturbing and sad. It makes you feel foolish, as if you had done something stupid. Why cannot a new love be like replacing the worn-out shocks in your old car? Why cannot everything fall into place, and life return to what it was before?

Well, because people aren't cars. And nothing is ever as it was before.

We will leave the two of you now, before any of us know what will happen next; you have some important thinking to do. Or maybe you think too much— you are never sure. Was this a moment that will take its place in your past? Or was it the beginning of the rest of your life?

4

Old Folks at Home

We were not married yet, but had been dating seriously for a couple of years. Q's mother had been in a nursing home since before I met him—by all accounts, she had been a handful even when she was well, and it took him several tries to find one that could deal with her. For those several years, her large apartment on Park Avenue stood full of beautiful furniture, but unoccupied—occasionally a friend might stay there for a few weeks, but it was mostly unused. One need not know much about New York real estate to understand that such an arrangement would not be the best use of anyone's resources.

So that Fourth of July weekend would be the weekend upon which we emptied her home so that it might be sold. I drove my car down into the Meatpacking District early on a Saturday and filled it with cast-off cardboard boxes in which we would put things from the kitchen and from the closets. Today the Meatpacking

District is an excruciatingly chic part of town, but back then you really didn't want to go there if you didn't have to. When I had stuffed as many bloodstained boxes into the car as would fit, I drove it all up to 79th Street and crossed Central Park to the East Side.

The furniture had several destinations: an auction house would move some of it, Q would take some of it and his daughter in Minnesota would take some. But the egg beaters and the lemon squeezers, the poultry shears and dishes, the teapots, the furs, old photographs and books, 78 rpm records from the 1920s, dresses, suits, purses and shoes—into the boxes they went, and into the car. It took a few trips, but by Monday the place was ready for the movers.

She had needed to leave her home long before she actually left it. A couple of attempts were made to sell her on assisted living: visits to this place and that place. No, no and no. Live-in help proved unsatisfactory, from her point of view and also from that of her professional—on one especially irrational day, she slapped an aide across the face. Once she invited friends to dinner at her club, only to forget about it and leave them in the lurch there, the puzzled maître d' calling her son for some quick advice on what to do with them. Her granddaughter hurried across town in the middle of many a night, responding to frightened phone calls her grandmother no longer remembered

placing when she arrived. By the time she was con-
fused enough that getting her out of the apartment
and into something else was an urgent matter of her
physical safety, she was also too far gone to enter
assisted living. Her options were limited to a nursing
care facility. Even then, it was necessary for the family
and her parish priest to stage an intervention and all
but kidnap her out of the place.

What was the reason for keeping the apartment
for so long? Inertia, mostly. Denial, too, I guess—it
was painful to admit that this chapter of the family's
common life was over. And, perhaps most profound
because it is so hard for an adult to acknowledge, fear
of opposing a strong-willed mother. My friend Her-
bert often says that most people don't change, they just
become more so. A lifetime of bowing to a strong par-
ent's wishes doesn't prepare a grown son or daughter
to take the wheel when the time comes. That is why
the power struggles we have with our parents in ado-
lescence are useful things, painful as they may be while
they are going on—later on, we will need the emancipation we win in those early wars.

Some people have an easier time of it. One reads of
elder communes: a group of friends combine to form a
family under one roof, and engage the professional help
they need to make this possible. It sounds to me like
they'd better be well-heeled elders, even before they

begin the project—in high-end shelter magazines, I have seen the gorgeous structures architects design just for them, replete with ramps, wheelchair-ready bathtubs, accessible stoves and sinks and dishwashers, grab bars on everything. It sounds appealing, though you would want to know and love those friends very well indeed before turning over a significant portion of your assets and all your at-home time to them. Take a few vacations with them first, maybe. And such an arrangement would require significant business savvy—recruiting and hiring staff, managing the accounting requirements of paying them. You all may go into the commune possessing such skills in spades, but what is the mechanism for the time when that is no longer so? Better have one. That's why assisted living sounds good to me. My guess is that hiring people and figuring out their FICA isn't something I'll want to do in a few years—I don't want to do it now.

Both of my grandmothers lived with us and died at home. The elder of the two came to us at age eighty and died of cancer at eighty-four; we turned the utility room into a sickroom, and a cousin who was a nurse moved in with us for a few months, relieved on some days by a practical nurse who was the mother of a friend of mine. This was a long time ago, and palliative care at the end of life was not then what it is today: her groans filled the house throughout the day and into the night. We used quilt batting to lay under her—they sold it at the general store across the street from our house, and it was often my task to go over and buy a fresh roll. I can still see its wrapper, covered with tempting pictures of beautiful quilts that might be made and filled with the downy padding. I daydreamed about making one someday with my grandmother, though there was no telling when that day might come, because at our house, the quilt batting was good for a onetime use only: we burned it when it had done its job, in a big rusted ash can out back. I remember my exhausted mother, trudging out back to burn another armload. I asked if someday we might toast marshmallows over the fire. *Not over this fire,* she said wearily, and I never asked again.

My other grandmother was younger than she, and arrived while she was still able to do everything she had always done. She was a magical grandmother to us, telling us stories, teaching me to cook and to sew, to cross-multiply and play gin rummy. She divided her time between her two daughters, spending the first six months of the year in California and the rest of the year with us. Her decline began while she was in our house, and there she stayed—a general weakening, a slowing of her step, the abdication of her household arts, one by one. This, too, was many years ago, and people with congestive heart failure could look forward to a future profoundly limited and likely brief.

She was my roommate. It has always tickled me that a social worker probably would not have placed me in that home if I hadn't been born into it—not enough bedrooms! But I loved sharing our room, being soothed by her if I woke from a nightmare, wheedling another story from her before drifting off to sleep. She was such a lovely person that it never occurred to me until I was all grown up that, left to her own devices, she might rather not have shared a room and a bed with a nine-year-old. If this was the case, she gave no sign.

The time came, though, when she was too ill to have a little roommate—my other grandmother had died, and so her old room was available now for me. The rhythm of the nights changed: the doctor came and went, my mother attended her through bouts of nausea and terrible weakness. Once I heard my parents bidding the doctor farewell in the hallway downstairs: he told them she had a fifty percent chance of survival. *Was that a good chance?* I asked my mother, terror-stricken. Yes, it was, she assured me. But I knew that it was not so. Every day I walked home from school filled with fear that it might have happened while I was away.

One night I awoke with a start—not in response to a sound, but to something else. Softly I made my way to the room I still thought of as ours. All its lamps were on, and light spilled strangely out into the dark hallway. The covers on her bed were thrown back. The bed was empty. I could hear my parents talking softly downstairs in the living room. I went down and sat on my father's lap; he told me my grandmother had died.

What was my experience, as a child living in a house in which two elders suffered long-term disability and then died? I cannot speak for my parents, who bore the day-to-day burden of both their mothers' decline and death—I know it was a heavy one. Even with her cousin's help, my mother had it hardest—once in a while I noticed this, but in the supreme self-centeredness of childhood, I didn't pursue it with her until I was an adult. I can say that I have always been proud that we could do this, proud that I could help even though I was only a child, proud that the two old women could be cared for in their final illness by people who loved them to the end. I felt sad, of course, but I also felt secure: my parents were there with us, and they were sad, too. But they were there. I learned that Death can come and live with a family for a time, but the family continues. And that was enough for me.

The draining modern task of discerning what to do and how to do it at the end of life is not unlike the current familial struggle about daycare versus stay-at-home mothering at its beginning. People have strong feelings about what is right, and the facts that life serves up sometimes conspire against them. The protocols of life's end will be different for different people. Like those of life's beginning.

Do I think that every family ought to do what mine did? Not at all. Not everybody can. Not everybody wants to. I can only guess at how hard it was for the adults, and for a family in which both heads of the household worked outside the home, it would be supremely difficult, if not impossible. It comes to all of us, this hard choice. The end of life is hard. All we can do is the best we can.

5

Most of Pain is Fear

It is now more than twenty years since I was struck by a car while walking home from work through lower Manhattan. When it happened, I tried to walk away, to keep on with the journey I had planned for that late afternoon—in short, I tried to make this unforeseen and unpleasant event not have happened. But I couldn't walk away: the pain of my broken bones was unbearable, and one of my legs wouldn't move. I sank to the ground, and soon the ambulance arrived.

I seldom think about it these days—my injuries have healed, and I can walk. When I do think of it, though, I realize that I still have pain, and that I have it all the time. Pain has become a constant companion in my life, like an unwelcome in-law who has come to visit and refuses to leave. And like such a person, its presence becomes a fact of life. *Over there on the couch? Oh, that's Jim's cousin, Francine. She came for a visit twenty years ago and she's still here.*

It hurt so much when it happened. Now, if I allow myself to think of it, I feel the pain, and it is significant: if I were to assess it on the pain scale they use in hospitals, it would be at Level Six. When I waken in the night with it, I am aware of how bad it is. When I arise from sitting too long in one position. When I have walked for too long. When it invades my dreams, taking the form of a malevolent being whose magic touch on my back produces pain. But during the day, going about my business? I hardly ever think of it. Why is that?

It is the difference between acute and chronic pain. They have different functions.

Acute pain is a messenger. It is an urgent command to the organism to cease and desist: *Get your finger out of that candle flame! Stop hammering—you've hit your thumb! Lie down at once—something has gone very wrong with the pressure in your skull! Stop what you're doing this minute—you're having a heart attack! Get help!*

Acute pain is your friend. It may save your life. Chronic pain is just your old enemy, so long present with you that you barely notice it any more.

My back hurts.

Yeah, well. Whatever.

The engine by which acute pain accomplishes its saving mission is fear. Sudden pain awakens our fear of dying, and we take steps to preserve our life. How essential a mechanism this shows itself is when one considers diabetic neuropathy, for example, which provides the brain with inaccurate information: pain when there is no injury and—much more dangerous—no pain, when there is. Dangerous: you can be mortally wounded and not know it. We need our acute pain to stay alive.

But does chronic pain have a purpose? Take away the fear, and it becomes something a person can live with and even ignore. Can one go further, and suggest that the physical fact of it has an actual use?

Maybe so. I think chronic pain teaches courage. Real courage, I mean, not bravado—it teaches the kind of courage that looks unwaveringly at the way things really are, rather than the strutting, noisy kind that asserts power it doesn't possess and control over events that human beings don't really run. No, the courage chronic pain can teach us is the slow kind, the patient kind—maybe "maturity" is a better term for it than "courage."

You may always experience a plummet in your blood pressure if you arise too quickly from a chair, and you might faint. But you can train yourself to do it slowly instead, and here are some breathing techniques that might help you.

Your back may always hurt in the morning. But here are some exercises you can do to counter that. You need to do them every day.

Your leg may always hurt you when you turn over in bed. But if you grab onto the lower edge of the mattress, you can use your arms to turn your body, instead of your legs.

You may not be able to genuflect by yourself again. But you can ask a colleague for his arm.

Or perhaps a deep bow will suffice.

6

Yellow Leaves,
or None, or Few

Remember when Mose came to visit us in Italy? Q thinks for moment, then replies cheerfully. *No,* he says.

This happens all the time—large segments of Q's life's narrative have gone AWOL.

I wonder sometimes if Q's memory loss will worsen quickly, if these frequent lapses are harbingers of frightening things to come. He's too old for it to be Alzheimer's disease. It's going to have to be just garden-variety forgetfulness.

But is it dementia? Only time will tell. Certainly, he is still himself. He can read a book. He can teach a book, for heaven's sake, and digest literary criticisms of the book he's preparing to teach. That doesn't seem very demented to me. But there are whole areas of his academic discipline in which he shows little interest these days, things about which he once was passionate.

Still, it must be said that the reverse is also true—he's always cared about the Israeli-Palestinian quagmire, but his distress about it is acute now, painful, as if he bore some personal responsibility for its endlessness.

We drive down the Jersey Shore on a brief vacation. We will stay in a town in which we have stayed before—it is our favorite spot on Long Beach Island. In fact, he introduced me to it; I had never been to LBI before I met Q. But now he is uncertain about its location, not clear about where Barnegat Light is. I am not sure he remembers the lighthouse, which is famous in New Jersey.

And if it is dementia? If this is the beginning of it? If he loses more and more, eventually ceasing to be the person he is? I remember the daughter of a brilliant chemist telling me that the love surrounding her father in the profound mental twilight of his last years was a testament to the person he had been. He could no longer hold his identity himself, she said, so those who knew him held it for him.

I can hold memories. *Remember this*, I will say, *Remember that?* Often he cannot dredge these memories up from the silt that has accumulated at the bottom of his mind. Sometimes they surface eventually, and sometimes they do not. But he is glad to hear of them—it is as if they were new tales, as if they were my gracious inventions. But no. These things actually happened.

We really were in Nice—you swam naked one early morning, walking right across the rocky beach outside our lodgings and into the blue water.

We really went to Virgin Gorda—we went snorkeling and you were amazed at the brilliant varieties of fish beneath the turquoise surface of the water.

Do you remember the birds in the avenue of trees in the gardens of the Taj Mahal? The Cornish coast?

Do you remember our house outside Siena?

If you don't, never mind. I can remember them for you.

As time goes by, I begin to wonder how much the historical truth of memory really matters. Maybe it is not as central as we think it is. How much does it matter, really, if a famous lighthouse slips one's mind? Reading a book is more important than remembering a lighthouse. Maybe what matters is not that memory is accurate or complete, but that we *share* memory. Maybe the central thing is that we hold memories for each other for as long as we can, showing them to one another, like snapshots we took on holiday. And maybe the importance we attach to the journalistic retention of precise facts is exaggerated— maybe sometimes a good story in the present matters more than an accurate recollection of the past. Maybe we can move into a place in which that is what we will share.

And when even that is gone? When we don't even have a good story? When I can no longer say that he is still himself? If a day should come when I do say that about him, I think that I will be mistaken. He may not be his former self, but he will be a new self. A self diminished in fitness for life here, but already on its way into another life.

We privilege cognition, as if it alone made us human. That is not so. Ask the mother or father of a mentally disabled child: that child lives in the center of their hearts, just as your children live in the center of yours. Love is not a reward; it is a gift. We do not have to qualify for love; we arrive already qualified. It is true, of course, that the complexity cognition brings to life is one of the greatest of human joys, but it is also the Trojan horse through which sorrow enters. Our capacity to reflect engenders in us the fraternal twins of hope and despair. You can't have one without the other.

Jim and I sit in his room at the soldiers' home. He commutes between the present and the recent past: sometimes, he and his lady friend still go dancing on Saturday nights, while at other times he weeps because she no longer visits. To my knowledge, he never journeys much further into the past than ten years or so— he never thinks his late wife is still alive, for instance, or his parents. Not yet, anyway. His dislocation, when it occurs, is often not total: elements of the present combine fluidly with elements of the past, as in a dream. He knows he forgets things, alluding to it often in conversation—*That's just the way it is when you get old*, he says, and smiles a smile I remember, the corners of his eyes crinkling merrily. What a charmer he must have been in his day, I think. He volunteers to organize a dance at the church; I accept enthusiastically, hiding the ache in my heart—Jim can't dance. He will never dance again. He needs a walker just to keep from falling. But the man who glided around the dance floor until just a few years ago is still Jim, still attracting the admiration of both men and women—in his imagination, it is all still his. Both selves are true: both his current frailty and the grace and strength of his past live together in him. Until now, the two Jims have been separated by the decades, each dependably locked into his proper place and time. Now they sometimes break free, wandering into each other's worlds and out again. The young Jim is full of plans and possibilities. *That's just the way it is*, he says a moment later, an old man.

There is no surefire way to make the slide easy, any more than there is a surefire way to ensure that your toddler will never have a temper tantrum, your teenager will not act out or you yourself will always do the sensible thing. No stage of human life is utterly predictable. Probably dependable structure will help him, and frequent reassurance about where he is, what we're doing next. A familiar face may help anchor him. Being alone may be frightening. His confusion may increase in the late afternoon and early evening.

 It is hard to leave this life. Sometimes the mind lets go long before the organism does, and insisting that it be otherwise cannot change that. The time comes when pleading for them to remember what we remember is nothing short of cruel. I remember when Q stopped reminding his mother that her grandson had been killed by a drunken driver. There was no need to deliver this news again and again, hurting her each time. *What news of Ross?* she would ask, and he learned to say with confidence that Ross was just fine. Willingness to ride with them upon the rolling sea of their shifting perceptions, rather than demanding that they endorse the categories of a world they no longer experience, is more loving than the truth-telling we admire in more ordinary times, and it requires real courage. We must surrender them as they were, while their physical bodies remain right before us. Sooner or later, the ones who love them best see this.

At the nursing home, Kathy leans toward her mother, who is propped up on pillows. She is explaining what's going to happen next. Her mother's thin hands clutch the blanket, and she gazes intently into her daughter's eyes, striving to understand. Kathy finishes her explanation. *Okay?*

Okay, Anna says, still gazing, and then adds, *You're my mother.*

Kathy absorbs this. *Okay,* she says gently.

SONNET 73

That time of year thou mayst in me behold
When yellow leaves, or none, or few, do hang
Upon those boughs which shake against the cold,
Bare ruined choirs, where late the sweet
    birds sang.
In me thou see'st the twilight of such day
As after sunset fadeth in the west;
Which by and by black night doth take away,
Death's second self, that seals up all in rest.
In me thou see'st the glowing of such fire,
That on the ashes of his youth doth lie,
As the deathbed whereon it must expire,
Consumed with that which it was nourished by.
This thou perceiv'st, which makes thy love
    more strong,
To love that well which thou must leave ere long.

—WILLIAM SHAKESPEARE

7

In the Garden

WE WHO ARE ABOUT TO DIE SALUTE YOU

I have noticed that many people who had scant interest in gardening when they were young take it up in late middle age. Something about drawing nearer to the end of our lives makes us seek out the life of plants. We find their mute ongoingness a deep comfort.

I will not endure much longer. This individual daffodil at my feet won't, either.

But this bed of daffodils will: they will return next spring, and they will replicate themselves, new daffodils growing up alongside the old, and more the next year, and still more the year after that.

Why do we linger in the garden when first we begin to see death at the edges of our lives? Do I seek beautiful and comforting thoughts there, to mitigate my individual decline? Yes, but more than that: in a life form simpler than ours, a useful allegory to help me live well what remains to me.

We who are about to die salute you! You remember this famous greeting, handed down to us from an awful place and time: the contests of gladiators, fighting to the death in the Roman arenas. All of them, gladiators because they were slaves or prisoners and the few professional fighters among them, would face the emperor with this desolate shout: stubborn and utterly realistic. Within half an hour, at least half of them would be dead, and nobody knew which half. This was their last half hour of life. It was time to stand and deliver.

From the Colosseum to the garden—a considerable distance. But death is everywhere in the garden as well. The plants face us in their brief seasons, flowering to get our attention and the attention of the pollinators they so passionately desire. *We don't have forever. Visit us now, scatter the golden dust of our encoded selves into the crevices in which it will teach itself to the next generation. In only a few days, our edges will brown and we will be no more. Help us do what we came to do, and help us do it now.*

The gladiators and the flowers: two sets of inevitable deaths. One is violent and horrid, while the other seeds life all around it. We are committed to that one, committed to it in so basic a way that we find its engines—the flowers—irresistibly attractive. We carry bouquets of flowers to our mates, or to those we hope will become our mates, tokens of the fecundity we honor, either in our hopes or in our memories. Their beauty is the only weapon the flowers have, and they use it for all it's worth. They use it all up. Good advice for any of us: you might as well flower bountifully. Might as well use up all your beauty here—its currency is only good here, and it only lasts a little while.

You sure talk about death a lot, somebody said last night. That's true. I think people should talk about death more than they do—or rather, they shouldn't shrink from the topic as much as they do. But we won't discuss it. Won't make wills or buy life insurance, won't choose health care proxies, won't think about what kinds of medical care we will or will not accept at the end of our lives. Won't think about heaven, about what it must be like to cross the threshold from one life into another. Won't even say the word "die," some of us, as if talking about it might bring it on. It's too upsetting.

But "upsetting" is what happens to a pyramid of apples in the grocery store if you walk by and pluck one from the bottom of the pile: you upset them, and they roll all over the floor of the produce section. "Upset" isn't really something that happens to human beings. We were never all that *set* to begin with. We get sad, sure. Scared, maybe. But not "upset."

We're messy by nature. Life is messy—messy, and then it ends. Nothing to be "upset" about—it's supposed to happen. We have to leave here, in order to make room for our replacements. The apples in their neat pyramid will rot if nobody buys them and eats them. They can't stay around forever. What good is a seed? None at all, unless it falls to the ground, St. Paul said, ceasing very soon to be anything like it was when it fell. What are your chances for remaining just as you are now? Absolutely none—and, if you did, you'd be monstrous, a person stuck in the wrong time, a living artifact of the past struggling to stay afloat in a present and a future for which you were unequipped. Nothing stays as it is. Everything hurtles into the future, faster and faster all the time, it seems to us.

That this is sad is a matter of interpretation. The more you think and wonder about death, the less tragic it appears. Christians are the ones who assert at least once a week that this life and this world, much as we love it, is far from being all there is. That there is an immense context to us, a context of which we are almost completely unaware, waiting to be discovered and experienced.

No thanks, says the seed. *I don't want to taste water and feel the sun, feel a tiny green shoot in my heart grow and grow until it bursts out into the light. I'll pass: don't want to become a great sunflower or a nodding poppy, an oak tree. Nah—just let me stay here in my envelope with pictures of these things on the outside of it.*

But the Gardener has other ideas. *You're going to love it once you get going,* she says, and presses the seed into the warm earth, sifting a little soil on top of it and pressing again. She pours a gentle shower of water on top and blesses it all. *Enjoy your next chapter,* she says. *I know I will—I can't wait to see what you become.*

Oh, my, I said as I stood by the window on a January day. *Aren't you something!* The new amaryllis on the windowsill just blushed prettily and did not reply. Two of her four blooms were out, and they were a delight to behold: large starry trumpets of creamy white, veined with a delicate pink that deepened to almost scarlet toward the edges of the petals.

Because she was new, we did not know what she would be like beforehand. We had to wait and see. The *amarylli* hold their cards close as they prepare for the great unveiling, the blossom-to-be sheathed in green, plump and growing plumper but not giving out any hints, working in secret on something wonderful that must remain hidden until it is time. Then the creamy white appears, and the tantalizing portent of pink. Or maybe it's another kind of amaryllis, and what peeks through the green sheaf of the bud is a brilliant coral or a deep red. It could be anything under there.

They are like us. What we will be is not always clear when we are young, which is why high school reunions are often a pleasant surprise: most of the mean people have mellowed considerably, the legend-ary beauties and universally-acknowledged hunks look more like the rest of us, and most of the quiet kids to whom nobody paid any attention have become compe-tent and capable adults. A few of your more delinquent classmates seem to have gravitated toward law enforce-ment. A lot of people look like their parents. You catch sight of yourself in a plate glass window and realize that you do, too.

In thirty-odd years of pastoring, I have seen many parents despair of their children's chances for anything resembling a happy life because of an inauspicious beginning. I have also seen many a young person start from the very back of the pack and finish well. No two of us have the same path, and some of the more inter-esting among us have taken very circuitous routes. So never write yourself off, or your child, no matter what. Never take any disappointment as the final word. We're not done until we're done. And we may not even be done then—who is to say what God has in store for us when we graduate from here?

For instance, common sense will tell you that figs don't grow in New Jersey. It gets cold here. In Italy they're everywhere: along the railroad tracks, at the edge of a forest, forgotten in a deserted garden, laden year after year with luscious fruit. But not here, not on their own. Here, you have to help them along.

This involves wrapping them in burlap for the winter
and unwrapping them in the spring. Rubbing the bottom of each fruit with a bit of olive oil in later summer, to hasten ripening—don't ask me why. We just
do what Luigi the barber told us to do years ago. Like
all Italian-American gardeners who ply their trade in
New York or New Jersey, the man knew his figs.

I resigned myself early to the probability that our
figs would not ripen that year. Number one, they
didn't get unshrouded from their winter cocoon
anywhere near soon enough—it was already summer when I got back from Italy for a brief visit. I
unwrapped the poor thing and hoped for the best, but
the long sunny season upon which an Italian fig tree
can depend is shorter in New Jersey, even if you don't
spend half of it wrapped in burlap. Then it was cool
and wet in New Jersey that summer, people told me:
the tomatoes for which we are famous didn't make
much headway, either. Fruits whose sweetness needs
to explode gloriously from within need heat and sun
in order to bring that off, and the Jersey guys didn't
get theirs.

By the time we got back for good, dozens of tiny
hard green figs had appeared among the leaves that
had hastily put themselves out there to catch what sun
they could. A hundred, maybe more, on the one tree. I
began looking for recipes involving unripe figs.

I knew that *The Silver Spoon*, the bible of Italian cookery, would have some—Italians don't waste anything that can be eaten, and if a hundred little hard green figs are what they have, they've probably known for a thousand years what to do with them. Sure enough, there was a recipe for unripe fig conserve. I would get some new jars and lids.

But a hard little green fig cooked in sugar until it softens enough so that you can chew it without breaking a tooth cannot be compared to a ripe fig: soft, sweet, dark, its rosy insides spilling out of a slit in its delicate skin, the slit made by the swelling wet goodness of what lies within. The fig is a lascivious fruit indeed, which is why medieval and renaissance schoolboys found it uproariously funny, and invented an obscene hand gesture imitating it. My unripe fig conserve just wouldn't be the same. September came and went, and still they hung, stubbornly green and hard. While making a conserve of our unripe figs would be better than throwing them into the compost, my heart was not in the project.

Such were my thoughts until I caught sight of something out of the kitchen window that took my breath away: a distinct shadow of deep brown on the side of one of the figs. And another, the same. Yes, they were on the small side—not much sexy swelling went on this summer—but they were ripening nonetheless. In October.

After about a week, we picked one of the darker ones and shared it. *Oh, my. Thank you, Jesus.* On subsequent days, there were more—two or three each day, then five or six. I'd pass the tree on my way to the train and grab one for the road. We were out there the next Saturday with a ladder and a large wooden bowl. Five pounds of ripe figs, maybe more. They were slowed down, but not defeated. This is what the garden teaches: conditions may not be optimal, but it's not over until it's over. Don't give up until you're sure it really is.

8

The Sorcerer's Apprentice

This computer can't make italics, Q says, furious. *My old computer could make italics. I must have pressed a button by mistake.*

Like many people of his generation, he believes that there are deadly buttons on our computers, buttons that will render our expensive machines permanently useless, others that will cast our half-finished e-mails irretrievably into limitless darkness. These buttons lie in wait on our keyboards, hoping that an unsuspecting finger will stray close enough for one of them to reach out and grab it. He goes to answer a phone call; when he returns, his work has disappeared from the screen.

I was writing a letter and now it's gone. He is beside himself.

What do you see on the screen?

Just a picture of raindrops. His despair is palpable. I was almost finished and now it's gone.

It's not gone. That's just your screensaver. I'll be there in a minute.

You don't need to come here—just tell me what to do.

But of course, I can't just tell him what to do. Computers aren't things you can tell people about. Using one is not a verbal exercise. It's not even a written one, which is why computer manuals are no more helpful than they are and why young people consider them packing materials and don't bother with them.

It's down there—see along the bottom? Click on it and it'll come back up.

It is difficult for Q to understand the significance of the difference between hardware and software. I try an analogy: hardware is like your paper and your pen, and software is your plan for what you're going to write with them. But my analogy, though a good one, isn't particularly comforting: writing with a pen doesn't vary from pen to pen. Pens all work pretty much the same. Computer programs, not so much.

Well, I can't write anything if this machine won't make italics.

No, the machine can do anything the program tells it to do. But look, you're in your e-mail program—see up there, where it says "send?" That's an e-mail you're writing. You can write more easily if you do it in your word processing program.

Long about now I begin to run a little low on human kindness—he is so frustrated he can barely hear what I am saying, and he takes it out on me. I am tempted to lash back. What I do instead is adopt a fake nicey-nice tone which is really obnoxious and must surely make him feel worse about himself, which I'm afraid is the idea.

Because it's not as if I were a computer expert myself. There are many things I can't do. There are other things I can do, but only in a clumsy and unnecessarily complicated way. I can remember being plunged into despair myself when someone asked me to send something as an attachment—*An attachment? What? How do you attach something?* I remember wanting someone to tell me, and I remember being told the same thing I tell Q: *I can't tell you how. I have to show you.* And it was hard even to show me. *It's actually easy*, said the person I had asked, and I wanted to slap her.

So, having been in precisely his position, you'd think I'd have a longer supply of patience with Q.

I always had an excellent number memory. I was the walking phone book in our family, able at the drop of a hat to reel off just about any number anyone needed. I can still tell you numbers from the past: our phone number when I was a child was 512W5 and, later 838-8309. My bank account number in college was 7-10468-1. But cellphones changed all that. It took me a very long time to learn my own cell phone number—I never called myself. And I must consult my own phone to find my husband's. I used to know all my doctors' numbers by heart, and now I don't know any of them. They live now in the memory of my phone, not in my own memory. If I lose my phone, I am on the communications equivalent of a desert island.

So it is with interest that I watch the progress on implantable memory chips: we'll have our phonebooks, our address books and, for all I know, our Christmas card lists permanently installed in our bodies—instant access, and *we can't lose them.*

This prospect horrifies many people, I know— *Eeew, you mean it would be implanted in your body?* I might have felt that way myself ten years ago, before I got my pacemaker. Getting used to it did take a while: the thing hummed away in my chest for months before I was able to shake the vague feeling of being soiled by the presence of a machine wedged permanently under my skin. I felt as if I might be something slightly other than human. The incision—crescent-shaped, like an upside-down smile—concealed something round and hard, harder than bone. I could feel the wires, issuing from the battery and disappearing into the muscles of my chest in search of my heart. I remember wanting those I loved to touch me there, to feel the outline of my electronic companion—it seemed like something they ought to know, as if I were living falsely among them unless they felt and accepted it.

In a year or so, I got over the fact of my pacemaker. Eight years later, when it was time for a new battery, my half-moon incision was reopened and a new disc inserted. I had the old one made into a brooch. And why not? Pacemakers cost about $25,000. My new brooch is easily the most expensive piece of jewelry I own. We'll do it all again in about ten years, if I haven't gone home to Jesus by then.

Of course, there are oddities associated with my bionic nature that do not apply to most people. When it is time for me to die, for instance, somebody's going to have to remember to turn off my heart. Another writer was telling me about an idea for a novel in which everybody had implanted medical devices—the bad guys hacked the system so that people's hearts sped up and they died. I myself have listened with more than idle curiosity as a pair of doctors played with my heart rate at their computer terminal— *Okay, now let's take it all the way down and see when it paces . . . no, see her pallor? So that's too slow. Now just take it back up. . . .*

So one more electronic guest won't bother me, especially if it gives me back my number memory and maybe keeps my calendar and some recipes. It'll do

more than that, though, I'm sure: I'll have complete
novels in there, mine for the thinking. Symphonies.
Movies. Complete recall of every conversation I've
ever had, maybe. Maybe I'll be able to close my eyes
and see all my grandchildren's photographs.

And maybe there will be something like Photoshop,
but for memories—maybe we'll be able to make our
teenage years better than they really were, for instance,
or our spouses handsomer than they really are. We
already know that there's such a thing as false memory.
I doubt that creating new, happier memories—or even
happier current realities—would be much of a challenge.

These improvements won't be free, of course.
There will be apps we can buy for our new implanted
selves. Certain competitions to which we have become
accustomed will be quite beside the point: we have
known for some time that the children of wealthy parents have an advantage in school in comparison with
the children of poverty, but that will go without saying
once we all have our implanted chips. You'll be able to
buy the SAT score you want. In fact, the whole notion
of schooling itself may be on the block—we'll just
download the knowledge we need, and pay for it. And
as for those who cannot pay?

The hair just stood up on the back of my neck.

The frustration I feel when I can't even turn on
our television. My husband's despair of ever learning

the language of the machine. The violation you feel when you realize you've been hacked. Your panic when you misplace your phone. Some of us, at least, already know something of how it will feel to be among the have-nots in the coming electronic age. The world will pass us by, but it will not have the courtesy to leave us alone.

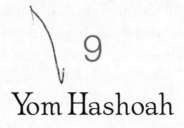

9

Yom Hashoah

The Jewish Community Center has everything: a fitness center, a swimming pool, squash courts, meeting rooms, saunas. Our Yom Hashoah program was held there on a Monday this year and it wasn't easy to find a parking place—the JCC is busy with many other things besides us.

We don't have as many survivors at the Holocaust remembrance service as we had last year. The ones we do have are old now—their children and grandchildren walk them up to the front of the room when it is time for them to light their candles. This year it falls to me to read their names as they come forward. For each one who comes escorted by a descendent, I add a statement about the great blessing their children represent. They are Jews: although the idea of heaven is not absent from their tradition, heaven is not their focus. It is the heritage of children that they count as their piece of immortality.

An elderly cantor will chant the first prayer. His wife, much younger than he, leads him to the podium: he can no longer see. I remember him from previous years; in his day, he was revered as a musician and worship leader. He begins the chant. I wish I could say that as he did so his frailty melted away, miraculously revealing his essential strength to all of us. I wish I could say that the notes were beautiful. It is not so: the effort of singing seems immense, and I find myself frightened at the way each syllable seems to deplete him as it forces its way out of his throat. What if he dies right here, I think, watching him labor, hearing the notes issue like groans from a place deep within him.

Oh, my.

Well, but what if he did die right here? It would be exactly the way someone like him would want to go.

I do not know if the old cantor plies his trade week after week as he used to do—I doubt it. He comes out of retirement for this observance of Yom Hashoah, remembering those terrible years that robbed his world of so many in his calling. When he can no longer do this, he knows, the link to those who instructed him in his art will be gone.

Still, he knows, he himself has ensured that the old melodies will remain. As cantors have always done, he has taught what he knows to those who came after him. The current cantor—to begin with, she is female!—is

a whirlwind of creative energy. She has a children's
choir and an adult choir. She finds music everywhere—
her choir teams up with the gospel choir of a Baptist
church in town to sing spirituals on Martin Luther
King Day. She sets ancient Hebrew texts to Irish folk
tunes. But she uses the old chants, too, calling them up
from the encyclopedic treasury of her memory when
they are needed. They are safe with her.

Jews know this about themselves: they are carriers
of history. If they will not carry, it dies in a generation,
gone with the death of the last one who remembers.
Some Jews respond to this by insulating themselves
from anything outside their tradition, though more live
in the tension between the old and the new by embrac-
ing both. It must be difficult, this voluminous task of
memory and exploration.

A memory of my own: a school friend whose
father had survived Auschwitz. He survived because he
had learned to be a tailor from his father, and so he
was kept alive to sew for his captors. With the greasy
smoke of incinerated human beings hanging in the air
he breathed, with hundreds dying all around him every
day, he remained at his machine day after day, sewing,
sewing. And he *did not* die.

After the war, he made his way to America and set-
tled in our small town. He did not work as a tailor
here; he worked in an office. He remarried and had a

new family—two children, a boy and a girl. Their lives
were like our lives in most respects: the same orderly
rounds of school and music lessons, sports and ballet
class. But something was different: their father sewed
in their basement every night after work, made all his
wife's clothing and all his daughter's, sewed into the
night after a long working day. And there was something else: the daughter grew thin during her junior
year in high school, every day thinner and thinner.
Every day she looked more and more like girls her
father must have seen in the camp every day, her body
an assemblage of sticks, her head absurdly large in proportion to it. I saw her once in the hallway at school,
not between classes when the hallway was crowded
but some other time, when it was just she and I. I can
see her still as she looked that day, the bright smile on
her wasted face, the beautiful wool plaid jumper she
wore, hanging on her stick body like a sack. Her father
made it, I guess, as he made all her clothes except the
ones she made herself. I suppose he taught her how
to sew. *Everybody should know how to sew*, he must
have said, and probably he said nothing more desper-
ate than that. But maybe he didn't have to. She went to
a hospital senior year, I was told. I lost touch with her
after that.

The father, sewing all night long to keep his world
alive. The daughter, courting the very death he had

worked so hard to keep at bay. All of this here, the war twenty years over. Here in America, in this land of safety.

He must surely be dead by now, the father. The elderly people who come forward to light candles were children then, teenagers or very young adults at the eldest—the camps were liberated almost seventy years ago. Life has been good to them since those terrible days, or so it appears: they are well dressed, surrounded by children and grandchildren.

⚜

What haunting they endure still is not visible to us. Theirs is not a generation that wears its heart on its sleeve.

10.

All My Pretty Things

Hurricane Irene filled our basement with a foot or more of muddy water in late August of 2011. It destroyed my whole library. Only a handful of my books remain.

Initially I was despondent—all those familiar spines, each one joined in my memory to a professor, to a paper I had written, to long afternoons in my carrel, hearing the quiet footsteps of other students through the stacks, the muffled noise of the street below. All those marginal notes, some of them in my father's hand, in the books he had handed down to me to use in seminary. My expensive Interpreter's Bible. The sodden manuscript of my first book, waterlogged and heavy as a tombstone, with all its editorial tags still in place, bleeding their bright colors onto its pages. My dog-eared copy of *Little Women*—and my mother's copy, and her mother's. Photographs, weirdly disfigured, their images separating into bubbles—half a face here, a hemline and a disembodied hand there, sliding off the page into nowhere. All my classical CDs. All my cookbooks. Gone.

But what would I have done with all those things, really? This house is a quarter the size of our old one—there is no place to put all those books. They would have remained in their boxes until I died, and someone else would have had to go through them and decide whether to give them away or throw them away. Hurricane Irene took care of that for me. And I never got a chance to thank her.

The shrinking of our living quarters has been an aesthetic challenge. I used to decorate with my silver collection throughout the big house—the large silver fruit bowl would hold a pile of pine cones or of evergreens, the little silver porringer sat prettily on a side table, the hodgepodge of small silver trays and plates alternated with the silver julep cups on the plate rail in the dining room. My mother's tea service fit perfectly on top of the little Korean chest in the dining room. The large china cupboard easily held most of the serving pieces, and my granddaughters' first paying job was keeping them all polished. The Japanese porcelain and the platters of Indian bronze, the Persian copper trays, the brown and white transfer ware pitchers and bowls—I loved all my pretty things.

I realized quickly, though, that these tiny rooms could not support much in the way of *objets d'art*.

Most of the furniture that held them all wouldn't fit through the front door. I could display hardly anything, really, and certainly nothing very big—it would not take much to make this place look like a fire sale at Sotheby's. Two years since the move and I still have not unpacked most of these treasures. I go very slowly in bringing any of them out.

I have found homes for some of them. I used to joke with my friend Anne about willing her my Von-Tury *Virgin and Child*, but why not give it to her now, while I can see how glad she is to have it? The reproduction of George Stubbs's wonderful *Zebra* would not have fit on any of the walls here, and neither would the Currier and Ives *The Favorite Cat*, but they made excellent prizes for a party game, and now they live in someone else's house.

Our tiny house has taught me to feel a modest thrill of victory every time I succeed in getting rid of something without consigning it to the landfill. I already feel a little sorry for Martha Stewart, with her drawers and drawers of measuring cups, her crocks and crocks of wooden spoons, her enormous hanging gardens of special pots—the poor thing has so much stuff! My new game in our little kitchen is seeing how little I can get by with—I have only the pots I use and that will fit on my pot rack, and I will never have any more pots. Never. I don't have dozens of measuring cups—only what I need. The Williams Sonoma catalogue warns me that I need one each of the twelve new sets of mixing bowls pictured seductively on one page. Actually, I don't need any of them. I have four mixing bowls, and could probably get by with three, or maybe even with two. I am considering this, because it would clear a twelve-inch square of shelf—I tremble with excitement at the very thought. I also think I might be able to mount my stick blender invisibly on the wall of a cabinet and free up some drawer space, and I tremble again. Every square inch I liberate is a small triumph.

A famous architect once told me that most clients believe that they need tons of storage space in their houses, but that this is a big mistake. *When you have lots of storage*, he said, *you just fill it up with stuff.* A good house helps you stay within the sane limits of how you actually live. And I have seen the kitchens of many of New York's fine smaller restaurants: some of them are tiny, with barely enough room to turn around in, and they manage to turn out superb meals for forty to eighty diners every night. Their kitchens contain only the things they will use. They are my new heroes.

This is like my first apartment when I was young and poor and didn't have anything anyway. I dreamed of having pretty things and a big house back in those days. It is like the later challenge of my New York apartments—New Yorkers know how to live small, but most of them bewail their lack of storage space. Rising to the challenge of smallness makes me feel that I am back there, only wise enough now to know that small is good. I feel efficient and strong, resourceful. Clearing this house out when I die will be the work of a single afternoon, I hope. That is my new ambition.

I do sometimes miss admiring the transfer ware as I walk by. And the Japanese porcelain. Maybe I should rotate displays, as a gallery or a store might— that way I could enjoy them all, only in shifts. Except I never seem to get to it: having fewer things around means . . . well, I guess it means I don't spend time fussing over the things I have around. I've grown accustomed to the ease of this.

Then there is the Christmas tree. No small children live in this house anymore; the small children in our family have their own Christmas trees. Church takes a lot out of me at Christmas time—it always has, but I'm older now, so it costs me more. In recent years, the intensity of Christmas decorating has lost its charm and has come to be more like a chore. This has been difficult to admit, but it is true.

When I was a girl, we used to visit people in the county home for the aged. I remember one old lady, who had a small ceramic tree with tiny lights by her bedside—oh, I thought this little tree was so sad! To have such a tiny one! I was sure that she longed for the kind of tree we had, one that filled our bay window and touched our ceiling.

I don't know if she did or not, but I don't. I saw a little ceramic tree just like hers in the Vermont Country Store catalogue and realized it was the perfect tree for this little house. It stands in the living room window now at Christmastime, elevated on a few books so it can peek out at the street. Cute as a button. I hang a few favorite ornaments on the dining room chandelier and call it a day.

11

Borrowing the Second World War

Loud thunder shattered the air and lightning split the sky. It was early on a late summer evening, and the sky was still light enough to see the road in front of our house, where drops of rain hit the pavement like bullets, hit it so hard they bounced.

Look! See the marching men? he said, one strong arm encircling my small body. I looked. The rain came in formation, it seemed, in orderly lines: fierce phalanxes of raindrops, like soldiers marching. *See how they march along*, he said. *See the marching men?* This was the image my father chose to comfort me, for I was afraid of the thunder.

It was the right image. The noise and the eerie flashes of light were not chaotic after all—they were military. *Army men*, my brothers and I called them. Our father was one, and three of our uncles. Army men were the guarantors of our safety. They had protected us so well from the enemy that none of us ever saw him; they vanquished him far away from our shores. Nothing could hurt us.

The blackout window shades were still up in the school and in some people's houses, but most folks wanted the light to shine in at last. The fathers came home, except for those who did not—Gary Burkins's father left their house up the road from our house and did not return, I recall. The young man who will marry my granddaughter next spring lost his grandfather on D-Day: the young father of a son he would never meet, a twenty-one-year-old who would be the father and grandfather of soldiers he would never know.

Everybody who could serve did serve, and those of military age who could not struggled against a terrible feeling of uselessness. Boys lied about their age to get in; sixteen-year-olds too young to join the navy shipped merchant instead. College students took furloughs from their studies to enlist. Some of them were young women. Married women who had kept house full-time went to work in factories to replace the men who had gone to war. On their days off, they baked cakes from strange new recipes: eggless, milkless, butterless. Their children walked around the neighborhood collecting used cooking oil and tinfoil.

Movie stars and popular singers hawked war bonds to fund this tremendous effort. They made films that

fired the hearts of their audiences with renewed deter-
mination and renewed willingness to sacrifice. Gone
were the glamour girls and top-hatted men about
town of the 1930s: the stories were sober and serious,
like the times. The stars were often in uniform—even
Fred Astaire put aside his tails, playing a draftee in
You'll Never Get Rich, a wounded veteran in *Holiday Inn* (1942) and an incognito Flying Tiger in *The
Sky's the Limit* (1943). The newsreels that preceded
the films showed young and old the war up close
and in motion.

Wives and parents dreaded a particular knock on
the door, dreaded opening it to see two uniformed fig-
ures standing there. Some of them fainted dead away
at the sight. Gold stars appeared in the windows of
the families who had received these visits. One mother
lost all five of her sons: they had all been assigned to
the same vessel. After that, the Navy stopped assigning
brothers to the same ship.

It ended, as all wars do. News of Germany's col-
lapse was followed by the slow trickle of unbelievable
tales of the death camps of Eastern Europe and what
went on there. Unbelievable, perhaps, but it was true:
there were the living skeletons in their striped suits,
facing the camera with hollow eyes. There were the
bodies piled naked on top of each other like sticks,
there were the prisoners kneeling in a line beside open

pits they had dug themselves. There were the soldiers taking aim.

Another few months and the Japanese also surrendered. It was usual in my generation, children of the Cold War, to hate the atomic bomb and all it represented. That was not the view people had of it at the time. *It had to end*, one of the old guys in my veterans' group told me fifty years later, shaking his head. *It had to. They would have fought to the last man.* The last woman and the last child, too: there is footage, meant to inspire the Japanese home front, of women and children on bayonet drill, lunging at imaginary Americans with brooms and rakes.

A handful of years later, another Asian war, a war uncertain in its beginning and in its end. Ten years later, another. Vietnam ached on and on to its ignominious end, taking with it once again the flower of a generation, as all wars do. Many people today call World War II "The Good War," to contrast it to Vietnam and certainly to our current conflicts. Me, I don't think any of them are what any sane person would call "Good." It was clear, though, and it was necessary. That much you could say.

When did our nostalgia for it start? I think it was in 1991, when we invaded Iraq the first time—that brief war, whose American casualties numbered in the hundreds and whose civilian and enemy casualties numbered well over a hundred thousand. The war from which we derived the lethal confidence that, henceforth, all our wars would be short and easy.

You remember it, I know. Enough time had passed since Vietnam that the people who had protested against that war were now middle-aged moms and dads, and had realized that the people who fight wars aren't the same people who start them. That the soldiers from whom they had distanced themselves back then were the ages their own children were now, and that thousands of people their children's age had died. In hindsight, their own pacifism sometimes looked a little more self-interested than it had back then, when it had seemed to them to be something pretty close to heroic.

Those who had served in the Vietnam War were determined that the soldiers of this one would be honored as they themselves had not been, and a frenzy of such honoring ensued: American flags were everywhere, along with yellow ribbons tied around everything with a circumference, in reference to a pop song that most people forgot was actually about a man returning home from incarceration, not from war. As a nation, we tried to atone for our failure to embrace those who fought the Vietnam War by doubling the volume of our applause for the veterans of Desert Storm.

There was more to our change of heart than atonement, though. The fiftieth anniversary of the Second World War crept up on us, it seemed, as big anniversaries sometimes do—*Pearl Harbor was fifty years ago?* people asked each other in disbelief, and soon the anniversary observances of American involvement in the war piled on top of each other in quick succession: Midway, the Philippines, Anzio, the Bulge, D-Day, V-E Day, V-J Day. We realized that the men and women who lived through that war were leaving us, and we hungered for qualities they had, things we knew we lacked: shared commitment to a clear cause, simple patriotism, pure hearts. They had been so willing to sacrifice so much; we, by contrast, could not seem to get up off the couch. By the time we invaded Afghanistan in 2001 and then Iraq in 2003, the contrast between our uncertain wars and that one was even more stark: young men no longer had to factor the possibility of being called to military service into their plans for the future. We had had a zero draft for almost forty years. The majority of Americans had no connection to anyone who served in the military. We were assured, instead, that the most important contribution we could make to the war effort was to go shopping.

Aware of our *gravitas* deficit but unable to remedy it, we sought reassurance about ourselves in superficial things. Candidates were roundly criticized if they did not sport tiny American flags on their lapels. The congressional cafeteria renamed its French fries: they were to be called "Freedom Fries" now, a truly cringe-worthy swat at the French for refusing to help us invade Iraq, one that would have embarrassed a seventh grader. More than a few bottles of decent Bordeaux were poured down the kitchen sink.

Some of us enshrined anti-Muslim xenophobia and called it patriotism. We wanted the ambiguous military adventures in which we were engaged to be beyond reproach, like the one that had brought an entire country together in a common purpose sixty years before. But we didn't want it to cost us anything. The wars themselves were not part of the nation's annual budgets, nor were they funded by our taxes. Nobody sold war bonds to pay for them. They were fought on borrowed money. Most families didn't feel them at all.

One phrase seemed to be everywhere, though: *Support Our Troops!* What that meant was unclear: military families suffered under the burden of multiple deployments. The suicide rate among active duty service members and among veterans skyrocketed. The aftercare of the grievously wounded was slow in coming, often, as a swamped Veterans Administration struggled and sometimes failed to meet their needs in a timely manner. Some of those who had brayed the loudest about Supporting Our Troops were nowhere to be found when it came to raising the money to care for them when they came home permanently disabled.

In some quarters, Support Our Troops was a euphemism for "Approve Our War." In others, it was a rhetorical device, repeated often as if in incantation—as if, just by repeating the phrase, one were actually doing something to help. It served to distance those who used it so incessantly from personal involvement in the actual struggle that characterized the lives of so many soldiers.

There were those who opposed the naming of the fallen on television or the practice of praying for them by name in public worship—Too political, a colleague said to me once. Really? That's political? Whether you approve of the war or not, somebody's son or daughter dies in your name—and you won't even acknowledge it in a prayer?

For shame. For shame.

12

The Two Baskets

What happens when this life is over? What were we before we became what we are, and where are we going from here? What's next?

It is as if there were two baskets, one large and one small. The smaller one sits inside the larger one.

We live in the smaller one. It is this world. I don't mean this world, planet Earth. I mean this universe. The existence we know.

We love it here, love everything about it. It is beautiful to us. Everyone and everything we love is here. The smallest crumbs of its history and our history in it fascinate us: we snap photos of it, haunt the library and the Internet to learn about its past, watch its birds and its butterflies, don goggles and rubber flippers to swim with its fish. We Google the Mormons to see if they know anything about our ancestors. We wish we could have seen the dinosaurs. At times, our memories of the past fill us with longing for it. Sometimes they even make us cry.

More than anything else, we fear leaving the smaller basket—most of us cannot bear even to contemplate leaving. When someone leaves, we count it a great sorrow. To us, the basket is wounded by the loss of even one of us; there is a hole in it, and so there is a hole in us. It takes a long time to recover. Some of us never do.

Baskets are woven, of course: strips of grass or straw or wood thread intricately over and under one another again and again, to create a concave form. But there is space between the strips, however tightly they might be woven. You could peer out one of those spaces, if you wanted to. Maybe you do, once or twice—put your eye right up against the opening and squint. Yup, there's something out there, all right. But you can't see it very clearly through that tiny opening. Besides, who cares? This basket is beautiful. It contains everything you need.

One day, though, the smaller basket begins to fall apart. *This is it,* you tell yourself, and fear grips you: this is the moment you have dreaded all your life, the one of which you have refused to think—this is the moment when you must leave your beloved basket behind. It is difficult. Painful, perhaps. But you become more and more intent on your leaving, impelled there, less and less intent on staying, until at last the smaller basket falls away completely and you stand amid its shards.

You look around you. And you realize that you have seen this place before.

Ah, now you remember! *This is the place I saw that time when I was trying to look out through the wall of my basket. This is what was all around us, only we didn't pay any attention to it. I have always been here.*

We have always been there.

When Jesus talks about the kingdom of God, he often does so in the present tense: not "The kingdom of God will be" but "The kingdom of God *is*"—*The kingdom of God is within you . . . the kingdom of God is like a mustard seed . . . the kingdom of God is like yeast . . . the kingdom of God is like a treasure hidden in a field.* The kingdom is not just a future reality; it is a present one.

And clearly, it is not a place, not in any geographical sense of the word. It's not a place to which we go. We are there already—*I have always been here.* Our notions of the life larger than this life are cripplingly provincial, utterly conditioned by the limited parameters of the smaller basket. The very term "kingdom of God" is an example of this parochialism, conjuring as it does the image of a royal court in biblical times: it is unlikely that the ground of all being much resembles an ancient Near Eastern potentate—or, as Jesus put it, *My kingdom is not of this world.* When we use such a term, we come face to face with the limitation of religious language, and are reminded once again that all of it is metaphor—the things of God cannot be contained by our words or images. At their very best, they can never be more than approximations. This is not to suggest that we should refrain from speaking of God at all— only to recommend a realistic humility when we do.

The smaller basket has collapsed around you. You are in the larger basket now, as you have always been and didn't know it. For the first time, you see it clearly.

I call the larger basket "the also-life." Containing all existence, "all in all" as St. Paul put it, the also-life is what you might have grown up calling the "after-life." But that term leaves us needing more: the linear timeline upon which the notion of an afterlife stands breaks down against the backdrop of the elasticity of time. God cannot have time as we understand it. We experience linear time here in the smaller basket—we need it to experience our lives, to experience the way reality works in a way we can handle. Here is how Albert Einstein described God's simultaneous past, present and future: *Time*, he said, *is what we have so that everything doesn't happen all at once.* What the ancients called the kingdom of God cannot begin at the end of an earthly time line. It must be without end, as you were taught, but it must also be without begin-ning—if there is a time before the kingdom of God, that cannot be the kingdom of God. There can be no time when God was not. Rather than a point on a line, the also-life must surround this and all other lives—it must be more spherical than linear. It must be like the larger basket.

Here is an image that may help: some of the stars you see tonight aren't there anymore, right? Weren't there when you were looking right at them. You knew this already, of course, from your school days. We only see the stars at all because they emit light—if stars didn't shine, all we would see when we looked up would be the blackness of space. But light does shine from them and travels toward us, and we behold a star. Except that the star we see is not the star in its current form—the light that hits our eyes left that star years ago, millennia ago. It took that long for the light to reach us. Who knows what that star really is now, at the moment you are seeing it. It might still be burning, but a lot of time has passed. That star could have done whatever it is that stars do when they end it all. It might not be there now.

You are seeing that star's past—in your present.

This fact provides a hint of what time is like in that existence that contains our existence. Linear time is earthly, and it is relative to the one experiencing it. Linear time exists in proportion to spatial existence: it's about getting from one place to another, from one state to another. Linear time measures change.

But say you are God, and hold the whole of the universe's history? What if you author existence itself? You, God, can experience no loss with passage of time, for there can be no moment from which you are absent. Everything for you must be now. What we know as duration is the stringing out of what is actually a moment. This is the only way we can hold what actually is: one moment at a time. We can't experience it all at once, so we hold it in bite-sized pieces.

Time is what we have so that everything doesn't happen all at once. But the truth is, everything *does* happen all at once. God can experience this. Tethered as we are to the earth, we cannot.

So? Is this approach to time of any use, or is it merely interesting? It is more than merely interesting for me: the elasticity of time is profoundly comforting. Here is why: we see everything in terms of our experience. My hearing a sound is part of the sound, my seeing participates in the existence of what I see. All things behave as electricity behaves: no power experienced until the circuit completes and then, there it is.

Now let us imagine the faraway star's experience, if our perspectives were reversed. Imagine a race superior to our own, on one of the planets in that star's solar system, a race whose telescopes were far more advanced than any we have—able to see the planets move around our sun, able to see our planet Earth, to pick out our location on it, so powerful that they could even see me. They would look and there I would be, sitting in the garden watching the hummingbirds feed, writing on my iPad.

Except that by the time they saw me, I would have been dead for thousands of years. Our house, long gone. This garden, this town—no more. The earth, too, probably. They would be seeing my past in their present, looking into ancient history and seeing it live and move: a woman of ancient times, living and moving right before their eyes.

Comforting, yes—because what is our greatest sorrow? That everything slides inexorably into the past. And our greatest dread? Sliding there ourselves, we and everything we adore—every person, every dog and cat and bird, every building and every city, all slipping away from us. No matter how we try, we can hold onto none of it.

We understand our lives in terms of a line, like the timeline your teacher drew on the board in history class—dinosaurs, then cave dwellers, then pyramids, the birth of Christ, the fall of Rome, the medieval period, the Renaissance—on and on, with an arrow at the end of the line pointing toward infinity. You mark your own life like that: *Let me see*, you say, *that happened before Mom died, because she was there* or *Let me see, that must have been during the war, because we still had those shades on all the windows.* The passing of time is never far from our minds. Our measuring of it is painful.

So think of it: somebody, somewhere, somebody far away, with the right kind of telescope—somebody could see us still! The light reflecting from us hurtles into space, crosses light-years and light-years, light-centuries, light-millennia—and reaches someone. Somebody sees you, when you are four and your mother is combing your hair. Somebody sees your parents meet for the first time. Sees your grandparents meet. Somewhere, William Shakespeare finishes *The Winter's Tale* and puts down his pen. The images of our past shoot through space until they are perceived. Yes, they are images. Reflected light. But we don't just reflect energy in the form of light; we also emanate energy. Not a lot—we are not very big. But we are composed of energy, the frantic motion of our constituent molecules and the motion of their constituent atoms invisible to the naked eye but very real. Energy holds us together, and energy is never destroyed. It may change form, but it does not disappear. It can be detected, however faintly, forever.

But I don't want it to change form! I want it to stay in the same form!

No you don't, for you will have changed form yourself. You would not be here to perceive your universe, even if it did remain in its current form. You would have moved on. Move on! Everything you have ever loved is in the larger basket, as it has always been. It is all waiting for you. It is all in the Now of God.

The dead are all there. You are there, too, though you do not yet perceive it: the you of now and the you of the past are there. The you of the future is there, too. Even the you that might have been is there, the infinite possibilities of your *youness* besides the one that our world knows, which we are naive enough to think is the Real You. You are not just the *you* of the facts of your life as you know them; you are also the *you* of its possibilities.

The good news—do you see it yet? What the also-life means is that nothing is lost. This is resurrection: not the resuscitation of only one small strand of your life.

It is the realization of all of it. And not yours only, or mine only. It is the fulfillment of all of us who have ever lived. There is no past. It is all now. World without end. *Amen!*